WONDERFUL WOLVES of the Wild

by Arlene Erlbach
illustrated by Jim Kersell

Dedicated to Sherry, the best wolf relative I know.

Special thanks to JoAnn Spieker and her adopted wolf, Kamots, and to Audrey O'Callaghan and her malamute, Sinead.

Copyright © 1996 by Willowisp Press, a division of PAGES, Inc.
Published by Willowisp Press, 801 94th Avenue North, St. Petersburg, Florida 33702

Printed in the United States of America   2 4 6 8 10 9 7 5 3 1   ISBN 0-87406-723-5

Do you have a dog?
If you do, a close wolf
relative lives with you.

Wolves belong to an animal group that includes

foxes,

jackals,

coyotes,

and your dog.

Long ago people lived in caves. Some wolves stayed nearby. They ate the cave people's leftover food.

People tamed the wolves. They hunted with them. They made them pets. These wolves are your dog's ancestors.

Like dogs, wolves are very smart. They hear and smell very well. Wolves are gentle and loyal animals. But wolves don't make good house pets. They need to live in the wild.

People think dogs are man's best friend.
But many people fear wolves. They think
wolves want to attack them.
This is not true.

Wolves are shy animals. People
frighten them. Wolves run and hide
when they smell humans.

Wolves live in a family called a pack. Some packs are small. They have two or three wolves. Some packs are large. They include a mother, father, and children. Sometimes they include aunts and uncles, too.

Wolves in a pack live together and hunt together. They play with each other, too. Wolves in a pack depend on each other.

Each wolf in a pack has a rank. The alpha male is the biggest, strongest, and smartest pack member. He's the boss. He decides when and where the pack hunts, and when and where the pack rests.

The alpha male's mate is the alpha female.
The alpha male and female stay together for life.
The alpha female bears the pack's pups.

Wolf pups are born in the spring. Before the pups arrive, the alpha female digs her den. The other pack members help her.

A wolf den has a tunnel in it. It leads to a chamber or room where the wolf pups are born.

Newborn wolf pups cannot see or hear. They drink their mother's milk. Father wolf brings food for the mother. He leaves it by the den's entrance. In two weeks the pups' eyes open. In three weeks the pups can walk. They can leave the den.

The pack members play with the pups and baby-sit them. They help feed the pups, too. They chew food and store it in their stomachs. Then they spit it up and feed it to the pups.

By fall, the pups look almost like adults. They go with the pack on hunts. They learn to hunt for food.

Wolves are meat eaters. Sometimes wolves eat small animals like rabbits or birds. Sometimes they eat insects or fish.

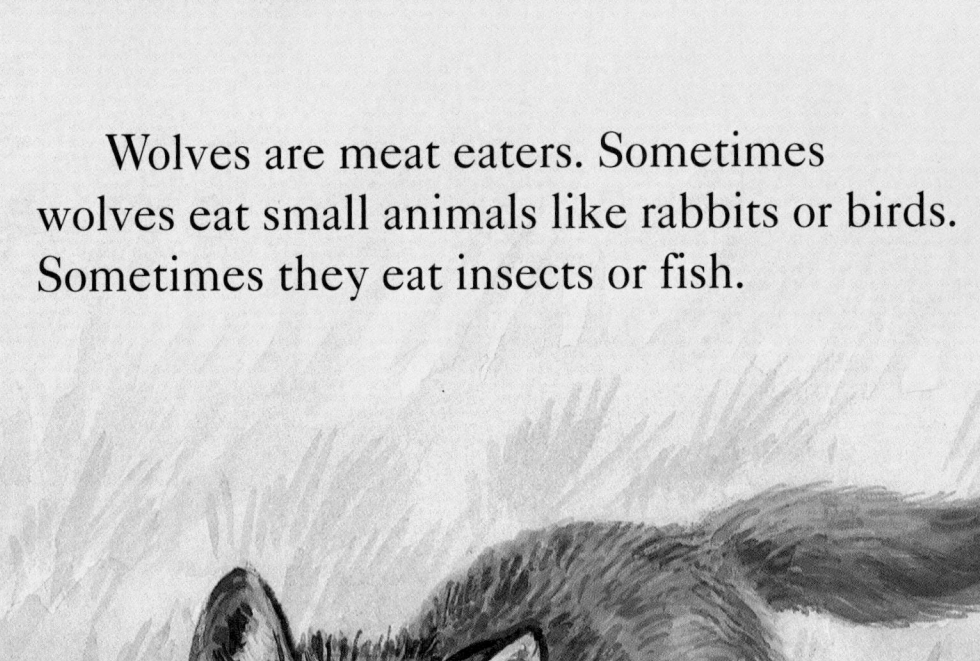

Usually wolves eat big animals
like deer, moose, or elk. These animals are
bigger than wolves. They run fast. Pack members
need to help each other to catch them.

Wolves are clever hunters. They follow a herd
and study it. They watch for a weak animal that is
easy to attack—one that is sick, very young, or old.

One wolf grabs the animal with its powerful jaws.
The pack drags it to the ground. Then the wolves
kill it and eat it. They even eat the bones.
Wolves do not waste food.

Wolves make many sounds—snarls, woofs, and howls. This is how wolves talk to each other.

A snarl means a wolf feels threatened. A snarl warns another wolf that it is playing too rough, or eating too much of the food.

A woof tells the pack danger is near.

Wolves howl to call the pack together. They howl to let other packs know that they are around. Sometimes, wolves howl just for fun.

Wolves also talk with their bodies.
A happy wolf wags its whole tail.

It wags only the tip of its tail before it attacks.

A scared wolf holds its ears close to its head.

Two hundred years ago, thousands of wolves roamed North America. Some people respected wolves and their hunting skills. They knew wolves lived peacefully in their packs and were an important part of nature.

But most people feared them and killed any wolf they saw. They thought wolves were a big problem.

Today wolves are endangered. This means there are few wolves left.

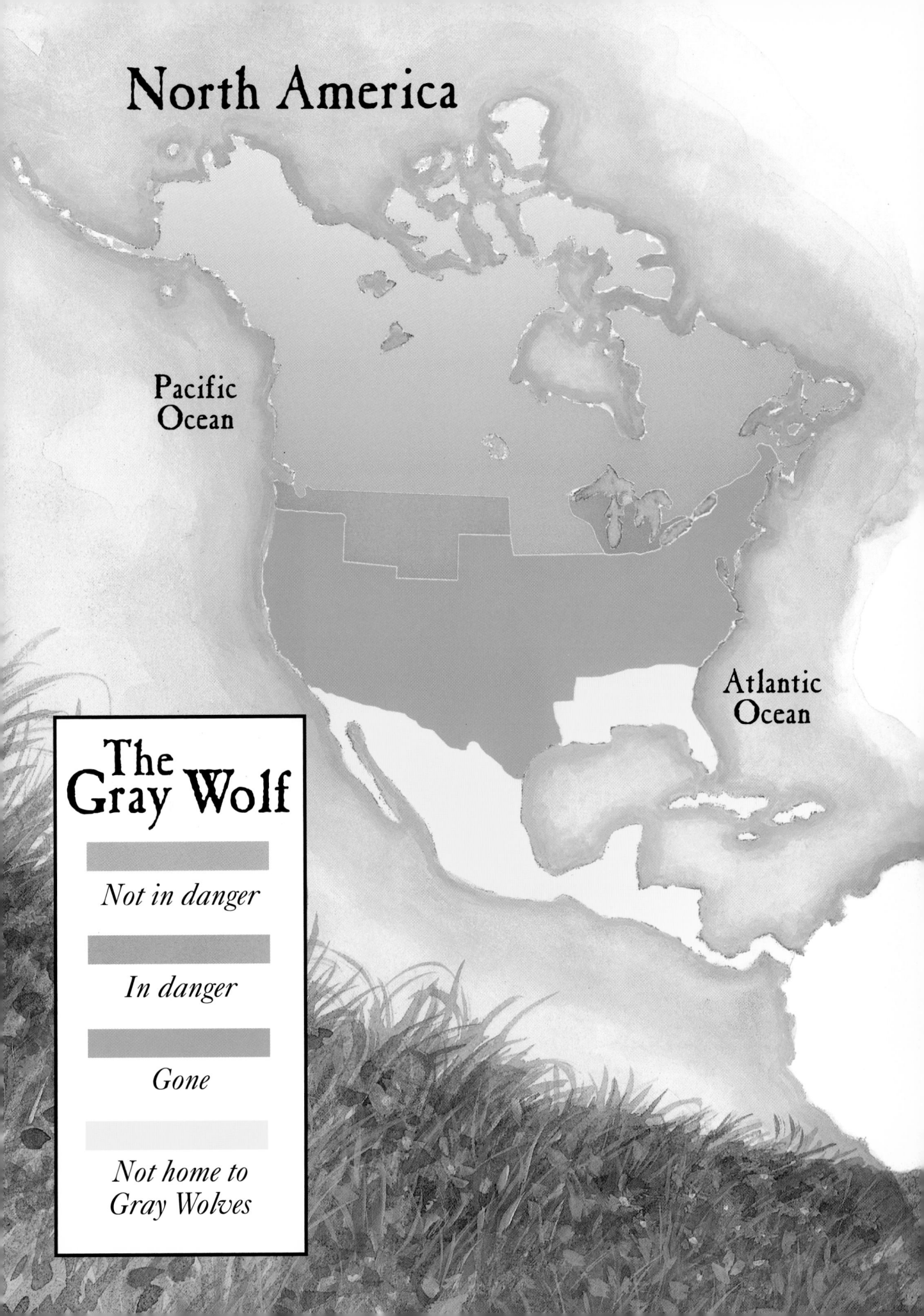

North America

Pacific
Ocean

Atlantic
Ocean

The Gray Wolf

Not in danger

In danger

Gone

Not home to
Gray Wolves

Now, laws have been passed to protect wolves.
In most states wolves cannot be hunted.

People are learning that wolves are not harmful.
People are beginning to accept them as part of nature.

YOU can help wolves!

- Learn about them.
- Tell people what you know.
- Write to these organizations that help wolves.

WOLF EDUCATION & RESEARCH CENTER
P.O. Box 3832
Ketchum, ID 83340
(308) 736-3860

INTERNATIONAL WOLF CENTER
c/o Vermilion Community College
1900 East Camp Street
Ely, MN 55731

H.O.W. L. (Help Our Wolves Live)
4600 Emerson Avenue South
Minneapolis, MN 55409

DEFENDERS OF WILDLIFE
1244 19th Street NW
Washington, DC 20036

CANADIAN WOLF DEFENDERS
P.O. Box 3480 Station D
Edmonton, Alberta
Canada T5L 4JQ